W9-BEM-564

Ten Steps Toward

SAVING AMERICA

A Practical, Powerful, and Compassionate
Approach to Biblical Citizenship

JACK W. HAYFORD

LIVING · WAY
MINISTRIES

TEN STEPS TOWARD SAVING AMERICA

Copyright ©1994 by Jack W. Hayford

All rights reserved. No part of this publication may be reproduced, stored in a retrieval system, or transmitted in any form by any means without the prior permission of the publisher.

Unless otherwise noted, all Scripture references are from The New King James Version:
 Copyright © 1979, 1980, 1982 by Thomas Nelson, Inc., Nashville, Tennessee.
All rights reserved.

Published by Living Way Ministries
14300 Sherman Way
Van Nuys, CA (USA) 91405-2499
(818)779-8400 * (800)776-8180

ISBN 0-916847-16-0
Printed in the United States of America

TABLE OF CONTENTS

*"In you
all the families of the earth
shall be blessed."*
Genesis 12:3

*"...I have made you a father
of many nations..."*
Romans 4:17

Ten Steps Toward

SAVING AMERICA

It is neither pretentious nor arrogant to propose that, though seriously imperiled, the future of America is salvageable. This nation can be transformed, through a people whose faith and actions are rooted in God's call and promise. Because the Bible reveals that, as Abraham's seed, praying believers have the potential to determine the destiny of nations, let us receive God's promise. America can be saved!

—*Jack Hayford*

INTRODUCTION TO HOPE — FOR AMERICA!

America's situation is not hopeless. If the living Church will rise to be the Church God intends, America can be turned around for good—and for God!

This past year, I have heard the above message proclaimed over and over by faith-filled leaders from different sectors of the Church. The conviction that America can be saved is not a concocted idea based on a personal, emotional opinion. Neither is it generated by excitable individuals with humanly-inspired notions. Not at all!

That's why I am asking you to read this message —trusting your faith and action will be awakened too. Because it's clear to me that the Holy Spirit is calling us…Together. Let's listen!

TWO OR THREE WITNESSES

The Bible says that *"by the mouth of two or three witnesses every word may be established"*—Matthew 18:16. Thus it's understandable why I believe this "word" about America. It's because the Spirit of the Lord is repeatedly confirming this message today through His trustworthy servants.

Just over one short year ago, I first heard this message sounded forth by a European: *"America will be saved!"* It was declared with strength and conviction, and the one speaking so boldly was Reinhard Bonnke. Literally millions have been impacted by this man's ministry to Third World nations, especially across the continent of Africa, where nightly attendance at some crusades has on occasion exceeded 500,000. Reinhard is a personal friend, and a man whom I believe is one of the world's three most effective evangelists. It was when he was speaking at a national conference in Louisville, Kentucky, that this anointed evangelist declared his belief in great hope for America. With resounding conviction, he asserted that God had told him that He is ready to save America if He can find people who will partner with His promise.

The second confirming voice I heard proclaiming God's readiness to "save America—now" was one of the Orient's most-gifted ministers. Leslie Keegel, the leader of the Foursquare Church in the nation of Sri Lanka, has become by any definition a modern day apostle under the touch of Jesus Christ. At another convention, Leslie said, "The Holy Spirit has spoken to me...," then, in almost precisely the same words the European evangelist had spoken, this messenger from the Far East said, *"America can be saved!"* Neither of these men had consulted with one another; a fact that should prompt ready hearts to see that the Holy Spirit is calling us to faith. Let us hear it, friend. America's destiny has not been resigned by the Almighty to the otherwise hopelessness of our circumstance. But God is speaking by many voices —even calling from beyond our borders to gain our attention.

And if these two witnesses weren't enough, God certainly sealed the matter with the third.

I was privileged this past spring to introduce Pat Robertson to nearly two thousand pastors and leaders gathered in Sacramento, California, from across the U. S. Pat's words were so much the same as those spoken by Reinhard Bonnke and Leslie Keegle, only the Holy Spirit's dealing could explain their agreement. No one has more decried America's present state than Pat Robertson, nor done more to pursue means of her recovery. But his words were not simply inspired on the basis of his own zeal or motivated by a private agenda. Though doing all he can to impact our nation's legal and judicial system by raising up qualified voices to bring redress to circumstances where contrived lawsuits have impinged on religious freedom, on this point, Pat was drawing on another source than human passion; speaking on the basis of a conviction born of the Holy Spirit. "Folks, God's trying to get our attention. America can be saved if there can be found a people who will rise in the power of the Spirit to be what they are called to be."

To these voices I want to clearly add my own— not as an echo, but as yet another witness. And my conviction is based on not only what God is saying today, but it's rooted in real evidence gained from experience. I have already seen what God can do to reverse dire straits of national circumstance when a handful of prayer warriors begin to intercede—and when the flame of intercession spreads.

AN EXAMPLE OF THIS POSSIBILITY

Nearly two decades ago, when *anarchy* was at high tide on our nation's college campuses, when the *Watergate* affair had destroyed the credibility of political leaders, and when the struggle over *Viet Nam* wrenched the nation's soul with division, dissension and confusion, a horrible hopelessness prevailed like a cloud over the land. The newspapers of our country raised the question, "Will America live to become 200?" —pointing to our then-impending bicentennial of 1976, yet a handful of years away.

It was at that time, during a mighty midweek prayer meeting in November, 1973, that God called me to begin addressing this national crisis by raising up a cadre of intercessors. At first I only thought it was to be a local call, in my own congregation here at *The Church On The Way*. But shortly, a movement was born—and we became part of a nationwide awakening to prayer—and to action.

Dear friend, what happened causes me to say and sing, "Mine eyes have seen the glory." God did something, because within four short years, America's then-disastrous state, likened by journalists to the crisis of our Civil War a century before, was mightily reversed. So great was this turnaround, the usually cynical and jaundiced stance of the <u>Washington Post</u> was altered: convinced, this journal carried a 1976 headline trumpeting, "A New Spirit Has Come To America!"

You and I know what that "spirit" was. It was the *Holy* Spirit—God's creative, redemptive power at work. When faith rises among even a small number of God's people, multitudes—*nations* can be impacted! According to God's Word, it is *right* to believe entire nations can be changed and spared when active intercessory faith is awakened.

HOPE AND RESPONSIBILITY

So, please, follow with me through these pages, fellow believer! This message is not soapbox oratory or superficial enthusiasm. I am (1) *joining my voice* to others of proven prophetic ministry, (2) *on the basis* of verifiable works of God within our generation, and, above all, (3) *because of the promises* in the eternal Word of the Scriptures! This is a message with a crucial truth for a crisis time. I'm asking you to open to its call to both hope and responsibility.

TEN STEPS TOWARD SAVING AMERICA not only points the way to hope, but it also points to our responsibility to act, in answer to the call of God. That call is clear: We are called to expect and allow Jesus to live in us in such a way that His footprints will be left where we walk. It's a call to pray in a way that His hand will be introduced in shaping power among us. It's a call for us to open to and realize the possibilities of God's unlimited potential in His people, spoken in the words, *"Christ in you, the hope of glory"* (Colossians 1:27).

What follows, then, is a ten-point outline for action. You will find it centers on both *spiritual* and *pragmatic* action. This is not an invitation to religious games: "Let's pretend and things will get better." But these steps point out a pathway with specific steps: action to take in the marketplace, in the workplace, in the voting booth, at the table of human reconciliation—very practical steps forward, in *faith* and in *works*.

Beginning now, it will take you about one hour to read this. Then, I'll ask you to decide to take these ten steps together with thousands of others I believe will hear and believe—*America can be saved…for the glory of God!*

Consider Step One, now.

STEP 1:

BELIEVE THE PROMISE

The beginning point for each of us is to make a decision. We must decide, conclusively and with settled conviction, that *real prayer-power truly is potentially effective* for bringing a saving turnaround to America. We must allow ourselves to be caught in the grip of the promise of awesome prayer power which has been underwritten by the Almighty God Himself. Here it is:

> *"If My people who are called by My name will humble themselves, and pray and seek My face, and turn from their wicked ways, then I will hear from heaven, and will forgive their sin and heal their land."*
>
> —*2 Chronicles 7:14,15*

In these few words, the Bible says healing deliverance can be expected. But it requires a certain breed of people He calls *"His"*—"My people."

God's people is a people *born* to faith. We are called "Abraham's seed" (Galatians 3:29; see vs. 13-29). The significance of this fact is that it reveals how *every* person who has put his or her faith in the

Lord Jesus Christ has been provided with a *genetic dynamic.* We have each been joined to the promise God gave Abraham, the founding father of the faithful. Trace this truth in God's Word.

In the fourth chapter of Romans, not only is Abraham called the "father of nations," but God calls him the father of *all* who come to new life in Jesus Christ. The Bible says to note the way Abraham lived and to live our lives the way Abraham modeled the pathway of faith from the beginning (Romans 4:12-13). We are to believe and act as he did—and the seed of his faith transmitted to us makes it believably possible.

Abraham received the promises of God, so much so, that even when everything seemed *dead*—when there was no physical or material reason to believe God's promise—he still believed. When things seemed *hopeless,* even as America's situation may, he dared to hope, and he believed unto *life-begetting power.* So, Abraham is shown as "the father of us all" who believe, and the Scripture says that now *his seed is in us.* In short, as surely as there are biological offspring, there are spiritual offspring—so we are believers in the Lord Jesus Christ; we're spiritual offspring of Abraham's. And thereby, irrespective of your or my gender or marital status, there is a life-begetting power that can flow through us, and it can recover a dying nation just as surely as Abraham's faith brought life out of death (Romans 4:17-21). Simply put, that faith-power can become a life-changing blessing to whole nations: for *"In you,"* the Lord said to Abraham, *"all the families of the earth shall be blessed"* (Genesis 12:3).

The most obvious fulfillment of that promise to Abraham was when Jesus Christ came of the seed of Abraham, as the New Testament explains by noting how Jesus was born of the seed of Abraham—and has become the Savior of the nations. From that point of prophetic fulfillment, then, we have learned there are yet *present* possibilities of nations being blessed. (1) As the Scriptures observe how you and I are the seed of Abraham; (2) Since Jesus has ordained His saving life and His delivering might to pass through us to all whom we touch—even nations; (3) Then we are to understand that the capacity to impact nations with blessing is inherent within every believer.

The starting point toward saving America is *you*—for *every* believer who knows Christ—to come to believe and embrace the conviction that God's recovering, restoring, resurrecting, life-giving seed is in them—*you*. Thus, those prophetic words of present-day hope for America, given by the Holy Spirit through respected leaders, can be received and acted upon by each of us.

America can be saved, if we can take the prophetic "word" of the Spirit and tie it to the timeless, unchanging WORD of the Bible—the eternal Scriptures. With this beginning point of faith, we can pray, "Lord, incarnate in me the faith to believe and the action to move." Then what will happen? I can tell you, because God has spoken.

Then America will experience what God promised —*"...I will forgive their sin and heal their land."*

STEP 2:

BLESS YOUR ENEMIES

The conditions in much of America's life today have caused many sincere Christians to become "fueled by fury." Some dedicated believers have been tempted by frustration then prodded to anger. We all feel this temptation, and that's why this step contains what may be my most difficult point to make. Jesus is calling us to be an *answer to* our nation, not to be *angry with* it.

> *"But I say to you, love your enemies, bless those who curse you, do good to those who hate you, and pray for those who spitefully use you and persecute you."* —*Matthew 5:44*

Here, our Lord calls us beyond anger, to *love*.

Our stance toward those whose decadence or rebellion opposes our best interest as a nation must be changed. Bitter attitudes toward civic leaders must be sweetened. We must move from a position of self-righteous, moral snobbishness or condescending anger to a posture of releasing love and intercessory blessing.

All who love liberty, embrace truth, and worship God have had many reasons for increasing dismay over the state of affairs in our nation over the last few years. Seeds of radical cultural change spawned in the 1960s, manifested in the sex revolution, campus riots, and the hippie movement, have now flowered to full blossom. We have moved from a slowly *diminishing* moral standard to one *locked* to a lower moral baseline. This loss of moral bearing seems to overflow into all the judicial, legislative, and social structures of our nation. Beyond a *casual* indifference to the things that preserve and protect life, family, home, society and nations, today we often find an *aggressive* opposition.

It's a painful thing to live through, seeing your nation's valor and glory pass its zenith and begin the same downhill slide that every nation in history has eventually traveled. To witness this downward turn can do either of two things to you: It can turn you into a *cynic* who surrenders to the circumstance, or it can bring *commitment*; lead *you to say*, 'I'll be a person of faith, believing that *at least in my generation* America won't slide from the place of blessing God would intend for it."

I want to say the following with utmost caution, because I don't want to offend. But I'm deeply convinced that *most* American Christians *don't know how* to respond to today's crisis. Though they believe in Jesus Christ and the Word of God, and though they embrace those moral values so essential to the preservation of any civilization, they've been neutralized rather than energized as instruments of change. This is because many have succumbed to *mirroring* the cynicism of our society rather than learning to *reflect* God's love. Frustrated with those who have no faith, we've often yielded to the temptation to answer "in kind." We grow angry or indignant at those whose rancor and rebellion assail our values. Prodded by others equally frustrated, we've often become a band of believers who too often take action that more manifests acrimony and bitterness than those traits required by our Savior's edict: "Love your enemies." For that reason, the praying *faith* of the Church is stagnant, and belief for the nation to change is absent. It's a principle in all of life:

You can never pray effectively for either an individual or a nation that you don't love. We can never pray successfully for a society for which we are filled with anger.

While anger and resentment may fuel zealous deeds, still both anger and resentment never have nor ever will generate any redemptive power in the realm of God's Kingdom. Intercession is paralyzed where there is anything less than a loving embrace. We cannot storm before God's throne in fury at our surroundings and expect God to hear our heart. Jesus told us in Matthew 5:43-46,

"You have heard that it was said 'You shall love your neighbor and hate your enemy.' But I say to you, love your enemies, bless those who curse you, do good to those who hate you, and pray for those who spitefully use you and persecute you, that you may be sons of your Father in

heaven; for He makes His sun rise on the evil and on the good, and sends rain on the just and on the unjust. For if you love those who love you, what reward have you? Do not even the tax collectors do the same?"

The use of the term "tax collectors" in this passage may seem irrelevant to us today, but please remember that the tax collectors in that ancient culture were considered *traitors*. They were people who had surrendered to a form of betrayal—selling out to an alien society against their people. Thus they were understandably hated by many in their society; not unlike the way some lovers of righteous values have come to hate those who have "sold out" for a lower moral standard in America.

This is so applicable to our setting, because hosts of us American believers feel betrayed by the direction in which some current political leaders are taking our nation. I understand that and I share the painful sense of regret and horrible sense of frustration others feel. I wouldn't suggest to you for a moment that I have not been tempted toward belligerency, anger, or bitterness myself. But I've had to work through that—to get to the other side of it, so I can become what the Lord wants me to be. And I'm inviting you to join me in working through and beyond regrets, frustrations, and temptations to embitterment. Let's rise to answer Jesus' call and teaching, being freed by the truth of His Word and the love of His Spirit to become and do what He has *called* us to be and do. Who will be willing to grow in the character and the love in the likeness of God? Who of us will be willing to *serve* our society as *interceding deliverers*, rather than as *irritated judges*? This process of growth isn't always easy.

Something I recently noticed illustrates this point, a problem I'm persuaded is a disappointment to our Father and Lord.

In a magazine ad for a Christian book club, I was surprised to note that even though all the books were usually only on biblical and Christian themes, this one had added a secular work. That prescribed no problem to me, because many secular books are worthy of our reading. But this club had made this exception for a specific *kind* of work—a book by Rush Limbaugh.

Now please understand: I have no argument to make against Rush Limbaugh; that isn't the purpose of this observation. But the point is that every other book on the list dealt with Bible or inherently Christian themes. The fact that the Limbaugh book was added to that list seemed to reveal something I think few American Christians recognize today.

We have become duped by the idea that mocking government we dislike is somehow a spiritual exercise. We've also been tempted to believe that resistance to the decay in our society can be accomplished by assuming a countering *political* posture, rather than prayerfully adopting a *spiritual* posture. The Bible points beyond this preoccupation with *human* obstacles:

> *"For we do not wrestle against flesh and blood, but*

against principalities, against powers, against the rulers of the darkness of this age, against spiritual hosts of wickedness in the heavenly places." Ephesians 6:12.

Again, please see the point. In the wake of Christian frustration over the declining moral climate in our land, I *am* thankful for vociferous spokespersons who represent more conservative values. And in the case of people like Rush Limbaugh, there may be reason to be somewhat thankful for some degree of national recognition of someone who has those things to say. Further, I have no argument over the fact that speaking out about our privately held convictions is our perfect right and liberty. However, there is a subtle, crippling factor that lies within any surrender to anger, mocking, or political cynicism. Anything that can neutralize my availability to act prayerfully as a believer in Jesus Christ should cause grave concern. An undue preoccupation with political analysis can beget a spiritual paralysis, and remove the true force of my capacity to change my culture. I may become *informed* by today's commentary, but at the price of becoming *deformed* for spiritual action.

Jesus Christ has called you and me to die to ourselves if we're to live for Him. And that calls me to a new dimension of understanding and patience with sinners in a sinful world. We need to regain the ability to bless our enemies: those who curse us, who spite what we believe and who work to destroy everything we represent. In Jesus' words—we need to love these people.

Why do I need to love my enemies? Because

that's what God did for *me*: The Bible says, "God demonstrated His own love toward us, (that's you and me) in that while we were still sinners, Christ died for us" (Romans 5:8).

Look at that! God had *every reason* to take a belligerent posture toward us and our rebellious nature, our sinning and our lost way of living. But the Bible reveals His great love instead, and with it, this great principle: *Where there is forgiveness, love, and blessing, a dynamic transforming release will result.*

God blessed us in sending Jesus.

God loved us in sending Jesus.

God reached toward us in sending Jesus.

In other words, God did all this *before* any of us made our first move toward Him. While we were still lost and blind, living in our own way, the Father *loved* us (sending His Son) and Jesus *interceded* for us (dying on the Cross). In spite of our decay, blinded hostility, and shameful sin, God did not reveal His anger toward us or mock us in our sin. He gave Himself, coming to us in utmost humility to save us—dying to His own interests and interceding to recover ours.

That posture God has shown toward us is the precise posture we're called to show toward the world. This does not neutralize our responsibility to exercise our roles as citizens in a free society where we have public expression allowed to us. I strongly support that kind of action being taken, and will later say more about how Christians in today's society should take an active, involved role in political matters and exert their godly influence. However, our *first* and *foremost* influence is *not* to be via a partisan, political position.

Rather, the believer's primary and therefore most powerful potential in influencing society for righteousness and moral justice will be through (1) *a disciplined attitude* of love for the people in that society, however frustrating their ways; and (2) *a dynamic advance* together in power-filled intercession.

Our first step is to faith, and the promises of national healing through those who pray according to 2 Chronicles 7:14. Our second step is to move on to the force that makes the faith work—the *force* of God's love. This step opens the way to making a positive change in the spiritual realm.

Then, we're ready for Step Three.

*An undue
preoccupation with
political analysis
can beget a
spiritual paralysis,
and remove the true force
of my capacity
to change my culture.
I may be **informed**
by today's commentary,
but
at the price of
becoming **deformed**
for spiritual action.*

STEP 3:

VALUE LIFE

When Christian leaders address the issues of abortion and euthanasia, they are *not* necessarily preoccupied with politics nor have they digressed from spiritual concerns. These subjects may seem to be only political "footballs" in America, but the real implications make the game one of Russian roulette…eventual death through disregard of moral absolutes. We are on the brink of killing more than unwanted babies or physically dysfunctional adults. We're about to kill an entire society.

At this third step toward saving America, I want to declare the absolute need for declaring our commitment to *life*. It's born of a respect for the Creator's world and devotion to His Word.

> *"Open your mouth for the speechless, In the cause of all who are appointed to die."*
> —*Proverbs 31:8*

There's no secret about this fact: we are at a crisis point in our national experience as to how future generations will value life—life at its inception or life at its conclusion. The imminent prospect of euthanasia's becoming legalized in our society is frightening.

In part, one can understand why some would claim to be speaking humanely when arguing for the desirability of legalized euthanasia.

Anyone who's walked through the death of a loved one enduring the financial agony and emotional stress of a prolonged suffering due to terminal disease has wrestled with every question along this line. But however understanding we may be, we're on dangerous ground to even remotely consider conceding to any humanistic philosophy which presumes to justify taking life into our own hands. We are designed to *desire* life and assigned to protect it. Always. Not only is man *not* to play God, by either unreasonably extending life or arrogantly shortening it, he is also to consider other consequences.

We can count on the fact that if once a legalized procedure for euthanasia was put in place, society would inevitably move to the next downward step. Motivated by human convenience rather than a divinely lighted conscience, upon the heels of tolerated euthanasia would be the practice of *early* killing of the *aged;* a step beyond a *terminal* killing of the *sick.* Some have already proposed the placement of "reasonable limits" on the number of years anyone should be allowed to live. Termination-by-appointment would be proposed, and in time practiced, to allow the "harvesting" of vital organs to service the needs of the living, sacrificing the older to extend the life of the younger. The prognosis: a society of wolves who gather to attack and feed on the aged and crippled in the pack.

Why do I believe this is what we could expect if we were to legalize euthanasia on the "end" side of life? Because on the "front" side of life, we have already demonstrated the human vulnerability to go from bad to worse. We began by tolerating abortion to some degree. "In cases of rape, incest, or the potential loss of the life of the mother," we argue the wisdom of the practice. But today, we have moved to the place where abortion is insisted on as a right— "available on demand," for the sake of any convenience. You can be sure, friend, our recklessness with life at either end—"front" side, with abortion, or "back" side, with euthanasia—is a frightening evidence of our moral decay, but it signals a spiritual tragedy too.

This isn't a sermon against abortion and euthanasia. Their destructiveness is so obvious to sound thinking, I don't believe there's need to argue the point. Because there's an even larger issue—not just one regarding babies in the womb or old folks at the end of life. The greater issue is that a nation which countenances these practices betrays a pathetic loss of *hope. We need to grasp that fact and let it break our hearts. It will move us past indignation to intercession!*

OUR SOCIETY IS KILLING HOPE
Our society is killing "hope." The bottom line

reflects not only a loss of reverence for life, but also the disappearance of a sense of hope for tomorrow. There is nothing that bespeaks "hope for tomorrow" more than an infant in the womb. And when that baby is put to death, for whatever reasons, that action is more than simply the taking of a life, as devastating as that is. It's a statement of hopelessness—that there's no other way. "Expectancy" is removed and death takes over. To see that will beget a *love* for our blinded society. You'll lose your anger for people, as you begin to see that we're dealing with a society that has lost hope—at the "back" end of life as well as the "front" end.

People who seek to shorten life at its end are not people who understand a divine *purpose* for each life. They're people for whom life's circumstance has become a frustration. It's not only seen in the baby that they kill or the later-in-life person whose demise they hasten. But the more devastating truth is that during *all* of their existence, their approach to life's beginning or ending reveals they have no hope for any meaning in life at any time. This national way of life, killing hope by violating life's promise, affects more social habit than we realize. Marriages are "killed" before they have a chance to survive domestic trials. Even people who know God's ways often give up on His promises before His life-giving power has a chance to grow fulfillment in their souls or circumstance. If you or I have ever been tempted to "give up" on *anything* or anybody—and we all have—then we need to let a renewed understanding concerning our national loss of hope rekindle our compassion.

Abortion represents a way of death that needs to be prayed back to life, not scorned as an unforgivable sin. People have lost hope, and in their emptiness and unknowingness, they kill the very seeds of promise that would bring joy to life if given the possibility to live.

If we can see this painful attitude of our society, and begin to love people who have become so void of hope, then we'll take the action we should—first, to pray. Prayer can begin to bring a harvest of people who will come to know the love of God, and then to once again love human life. But to expect the latter without the former is to fail to see how "without hope and without God" our dear America has become (Read Ephesians 2:11-17, for "hope").

GIVING HOPE

When *our* hearts begin to see *the* heart of the problem, and when we put prayer first and remove judgment from the picture, then we can take additional action which "values life." Here are some things we can do in *love*, rather than in criticism for our society's disregard for life:

1. *Provide literature with "Hope."*

   I've written a little book entitled, I'LL HOLD YOU IN HEAVEN. The reason I wrote this book was to give hope to people who have had an abortion. It's also become a book of hope for couples who have lost children through uncalculated natural abortions such as miscarriages or stillbirths.

The Bible reveals to us that there is the most joyous and thrilling possibility that these people will be holding those children in heaven some day: it's revealed in God's Word! I believe the exposition of that theme is something that deserves to be spread; to be disseminated by people who would take hope-inspiring truth to those who have suffered the loss of a child.

You can do as others have: Give or distribute material like this. Many copies of this book have been distributed across the nation and given to women who come into Crisis Pregnancy Centers, as well as to men who have participated in abortions. As these people return to sanity, realizing the sanctity of life, something like this book helps them deal with the pain as well as the eternal realities of life in a context of hope.

I'm not suggesting I'LL HOLD YOU IN HEAVEN is the only resource for such ministry. But I want to encourage you to see how we can help people regain hope who have earlier lost it and surrendered to the world's "death" system. Such people need to find out that God's loving answer not only brings them forgiveness, but it offers *hope*—hope for a future which will even include the embracing of that child they lost or aborted.

2. *Point to the wisdom of the respected.*

One of the most meaningful gifts I received on the occasion which recently honored my wife's and my 25 years of pastoral leadership at The Church On The Way, was a simple letter. It was a personal note from Mother Teresa, in Calcutta, who said, "I thank God for all the good He has done in you and through you…and I pray for you…May God bless you to continue His work with greater love and zeal."

I was humbled and blessed, because she is unquestionably one of today's greatest and most respected servants to humanity. The whole world positively acknowledges such people, because the inescapable practicality of their devotion commands universal respect. Thus, to enunciate, to our peers or associates, the *words* of a Mother Teresa, becomes an irresistible point, appropriately spoken in a gentle way that can be received.

Let me relate how, at the 1994 National Prayer Breakfast in Washington, D. C., Mother Teresa spoke to over four thousand people, including our President of the United States. As she first simply, but profoundly presented the message of the Gospel, she went on to tell the crowd of Jesus' love: "He died for you and for me, and for that leper and for that man dying of hunger and that naked person lying in the street, not only of Calcutta, but of Africa, and everywhere."

Then, continuing by showing that Jesus brought love to us in coming as a child, she stressed how each child has been created in the image of God to know that love; that when we embrace a child, we contribute to the same kind of possibility of peace in that child that the Son of God, coming as a child, brought to us. Then she said:

"But I feel the greatest destroyer of peace today is abortion. The killing of an innocent child is a way of saying it's all right to kill each other." Then, with grace and gentleness, she pled: "Please don't kill the child. I want the child. Please give the child to me." She called believers to be available to adopt unwanted children, as she further urged positive actions for dealing with this problem in our world.

This vital example of "speaking the truth in love" (Ephesians 4:15) shows how we can oppose the desecration of life without becoming an adversary to the blinded, hopeless people who blindly walk in dark ways. And these words provide wisdom, wisely spoken, which we can relay to others.

3. *Share beautiful testimonies.*

We can help remind our society of life's preciousness in other ways than attacking those we disagree with. For example, the DeMoss Foundation has funded a masterfully, poignant series of TV commercials themed "Life—What a beautiful choice!" Also, the warm and wonderful testimonies of people who have bypassed abortion can be related without condemnation.

I recently invited a remarkable young woman to share with our congregation as a part of a Sunday morning service. Gianna Jessen is a beautiful, talented teenager today, in spite of the fact that 17 years ago her natural mother tried to abort her by saline injection. Miraculously she survived, and she was placed in an institution. The prognosis there was that the side-effects of the attempted abortion assured the baby would not survive; that even if it did, it would be hopelessly and permanently handicapped. However, a woman came into this child's life. She adopted the damaged infant, and through superhuman patience and supernatural love, she turned the tables on these predictions. By one person's *not letting go of her hope* that God had a purpose and a plan for this child's life, we have Gianna's testimony today. It's a beautiful statement of God's saying, "I will intervene even in the midst of the most drastic circumstances to raise up a testimony of how much I want to preserve life." Gianna's adoptive mother is also a beautiful statement.

How dramatic a picture of what an adoptive parent can mean to the possibility of a child coming into meaningful life! Gianna Jessen is a lovely, gifted, young woman now, notwithstanding a physical handicap. Even though birthed in burning agony, and handed an absolutely futile beginning, by a miracle of the grace of God, her testimony shines forth of God's high value placed on human life.

STEP 4:

LOVE THE BODY

My desire is to draw us all toward a development or deepening of that spirit Paul sought to engender in the Early Church. In such passages as 1 Corinthians 12, where he urges attention toward the preciousness of the place each of us holds in the Body of Christ, he appeals to our loving all members of Christ's body. To the Romans he gave these guidelines for graciousness to each other:

> *"For I say, through the grace given to me, to everyone who is among you, not to think of himself more highly than he ought to think, but to think soberly, as God has dealt to each one a measure of faith."* —Romans 12:3

Mutual respect and acceptance among all God's redeemed family are absolutely essential today, if we would win a nation. But such unity requires an end of suspicion, criticism, judgmentalism, and separatism.

The longer I serve as a shepherd to the flock of

our Lord Jesus, the more I become pained by the reality of the "wolf-spirit" Paul described, which lurks about, seeking to savage God's sheep (Acts 20:28-30). He noted that even among the Lord's people are many who care more for their own agenda than for God's; who pride themselves in their own supposed righteousness, and seize any issue to justify their attack on the seeming imperfection of others.

Jesus' prayer is so readily overlooked: "That they may all be one, Father, even as we are one…That the world may know that You have sent Me" (John 17:21). Loved one, if our land is to be fully impacted for God, good, and the Gospel, we must all come to "love the Body of Christ"—that is, receive and accept one another. But too often, otherwise is seen all around us.

I wish every reader could see the video presentation of this message you are reading. As I delivered this sermon, I was caught in a moment of inspiration and dramatized the horrible, crippling effect of division in Christ's Body. The following words attempt to communicate that "picture," though I wish you could see the telecast of "Ten Steps Toward Saving America."*

Picture in your mind, if you will, a deformed person, unable to stand straight because of his disability. He is horribly stooped—his back, arms, and legs all bent at awkward angles. Because there is so much muscle tension in his body, he can hardly move. What movements he is able to make are stiff and jerky, the best his shrunken, uncoordinated body can perform.

I believe this is a picture of the Body of Christ in America today. Because of the tensions existing within it—because of criticism, anger, suspicion, jealousy, pride, and the like, only limited movement forward is possible. But if the Body of Christ will turn from its crippling habits, repent of them and release the spirit of unity, we can still rise in strength to become what the Lord wants us to be.

But small-souled, nit-picking must end. Those who have felt their main task is to "watchdog" the Body of Christ must cease their critical judgments in the publishing and broadcasting communities. The "junkyard watchdog" mentality of snarling antagonism has no place. The Body of Christ needs watch*men*, but it doesn't need watch*dogs*.

Let's allow a fresh baptism of love to overflow us all; removing all smallness that would separate us.

Loved one, do you find yourself capable of criticizing or looking down upon anyone in the Church of Jesus who is different from you in worship, perspective, or doctrine? The Savior is calling you and me to be people who love His Church. Jesus is saying, "Love Me. Love My bride."

The spirit of Step Four logically will lead to Step Five. Unity will advance much needed reconciliation even where unperceived barricades to unity exist. Beyond the blockages of doctrinal, denominational and sectarian division, we must heed God's call to *trans-ethnic* love.

The Church must model love at *every* point, if she is to rise in spiritual power to affect America.

*Information on securing audio or video tapes of "Ten Steps Toward Saving America," may be found on page 92.

STEP 5:

PURSUE PEACE

The embracing of every ethnic group is required by the mandate of the Creator, Who "has made from one blood all nations of men to dwell on the earth" (Acts 17:26). In an America still rife with ethnic division, interracial animosities and the residue of systemic racism which still badgers our efforts at securing equality for all citizens, the Church has an immeasurably grand opportunity. Here is her chance to *shine*, manifesting the spirit of unity which characterized the Church the day it was born (see Acts 2:8-11). Too often however the Church is only *mirroring* the culture's values rather than *lighting* the way. If we are going to impact America with God's justice and love—which always work in tandem—then the Church's manifest leadership in trans-ethnic reconciliation is God's order for all of us as believers. The Bible clearly says such "peace" must be sought —worked at earnestly.

> *"Depart from evil and do good; Seek peace and pursue it."*
>
> *"Let him turn away from evil and do good; Let*

him seek peace and pursue it."
                    —Psalm 34:14; 1 Peter 3:11

Billy Graham was recently asked by an interviewer, "What is the greatest single problem in the world as you see it?" Without hesitation, Dr. Graham answered that he sees the greatest problem in our world today as racism, with the strife, hatred, dissension and stress that are brought about by it.

I thoroughly believe that the Church has been called to model trans-ethnic (i.e., inter-racial) reconciliation. According to the Scriptures, there's only one race, as we've seen in Acts 17:26: "One blood" emphasizes the unity of the human race as no other expression can. And, as a biological fact, it settles the case conclusively: Skin tones and cultures vary, but in *God's* order and in the biological order, all mankind are one people—one race named "Human." If you're dying, in need of a blood transfusion, I doubt it would make any difference to any of us what color, race, or ethnic group our donor comes from. When life is at stake, so small a matter as "racial/ethnic derivation" means nothing to us. And, dear friend, that's exactly where we are today. America's life is at stake—as well as the *true* life of Christ as revealed through His Church by the love of God. The hour calls for serious, self-sacrificing attention to this subject.

The depth of the variety in our humanity and in our cultures was never intended by God to *divide*. Under His order, it was intended to *provide* a beautiful canvas of variety and interest. However, fallen man being what he is, we still have the traits and taints of that fallenness in us. Even though we have been forgiven of our sins, sometimes those taints continue to influence us. Too often we have been shaped so completely by our cultural surroundings, we succumb to the temptation to sanctify or justify our prejudices.

If Pentecost shows us anything at the Church's inception, it's that the Lord Jesus birthed the Church to become a trans-ethnic group which would melt down the barriers of racial strife and bitterness in the world. Unfortunately, the Church hasn't done well in assuming that role.

The Church of Jesus Christ can have little credibility to a culture when it only reflects the prejudices of that culture. We've been called to be a people who show the love of God for everybody and learn how to live out that way of life at every social as well as spiritual dimension.

To impact America with the kind of "model" the Church ought to demonstrate—how ethnic/racial differences are transcended in God's Kingdom of love—discernment is needed. To be *distinctive* in our model, we'll need to be able to *distinguish* between the world's best efforts and God's better way.

POLITICAL CORRECTNESS VS. KINGDOM CORRECTNESS

For example, there is a considerable amount of

concern over maintaining a stance of "political correctness" in America today in society's methods, manners and speech. Among these "means" of striving for human harmony, "political correctness" requires "ethnic quotas." In other words, if you have a mixture of groups in an institution, in a gathering, in an organization, then there has to be a "certain" number or percentage of each ethnic or gender group to meet acceptability. I'm not impugning the social goals in view through such quests, however, being "politically correct" is not a divine prescription for social solutions. Rather, God calls mankind to Kingdom rebirth, and *then* "Kingdom correctness"—i.e., doing things God's way by God's Spirit, treating every human being with respect and dignity as a member of God's creation. This transcends quotas and carefully guarded words, though it may include carefulness toward these issues as considerations. But, well beyond that, we need a changing of our hearts! Let me give a very practical illustration from the life of my own church's congregation.

The Church Council at *The Church On The Way* is comprised of nine members. Each serves a three-year term, and three members are elected each year. On our last ballot for Church Councilmen there were six candidates nominated to fill the three Council seats coming open. Of the six, five were Caucasian and one was Asian. Several days after the balloting, someone in our congregation said to one of our pastors (without any malice), "You know, I was kind of sorry not to see a Hispanic on the ballot."

They didn't mention what they already knew, that our Church Council *happens* to already have a Hispanic (and an African-American too, for that matter). They were solely making the observation as a result of the societal influences that surround today—the "quota" requirements. What they forgot was that none of the men who were candidates for our Council are selected for *ethnic* reasons, but for *spiritual* ones. We honor social concerns for fairness toward all, but refuse to "play to" some humanly designed order of a politically correct "representative" system.

Our Elders, who govern all the affairs of our congregation, aren't made candidates for their position because they have a certain ethnicity any more than we would place them in office for reasons of their financial wealth or social status. "Clout" or moneyed position has nothing to do with God's practices. Our leaders sit in governing positions for *"Kingdom correct"* reasons. They are people (1) who have been proven as *servant-spirited* members of the body of the congregation for years and years; (2) who have verified by their attitude and practice that they understand the life and the spirit of Jesus at work in this church, and (3) they are committed to the ways of Christ, as faithful discipleship is seen in every part of their lives.

It takes a long time to disciple a man or a woman of that "Kingdom" quality. It takes growth in God's Word and the love of God's Spirit, and no human "quota" system can dictate God's pace for growing leaders. So, our procedures flow from a respect for the kind of person a leader is to be in Christ. Yet even though we resist human schemes of ethnic quotas, we still demonstrate a lifestyle which transcends ethnic separatism, debate, and animosity. It makes for a much "louder" and believable voice to the world at our doors, and, incidentally, we *do* have a *very* representative constituency on our Council *ethnically* as well! But by God's *grace* in people, not by human mandate or system.

America needs models of how God's love brings people together. And I believe the lost will naturally gravitate to places where *political* correctness and *Kingdom* correctness are seen for what they are—worlds apart, with the latter proving infinitely more effective, loving, life-begetting, and unifying.

Within the Church we must face this fact: if we would offer "saving" life to America, we must demonstrate trans-ethnic understanding and reconciliation. Until men's hearts and attitudes are changed by their willingness to confront those attitudes and see them changed by the Holy Spirit's power, the Church will not be the instrument in God's hands that He would have it be.

Footnote:

I have dealt with this subject extensively in a video series, entitled "Outracing the World." In that series, I presented an in-depth study of the attitudes in all of us that need to be confronted if we're going to become the people of the Lord who pursue peace and become instruments of reconciliation in the world.

*If Pentecost
shows us anything at
the Church's inception,
it's that the Lord
birthed the Church
to become
a trans–ethnic group
which would melt down
the barriers
of racial strife
and bitterness
in the world.*

STEP 6:

LIVE IN PURITY

The Word of God, lived out by the early Church, showed that the way to assert moral superiority in a corrupt culture is to shine by example, not shoot as an adversary.

> *"Do all things without complaining and disput-*
> *ing, that you may become blameless and harm-*
> *less, children of God without fault in the midst of*
> *a crooked and perverse generation, among whom*
> *you shine as lights in the world."*
> —*Philippians 2:14-15*

In Philippians, Paul is writing to people who lived in one of the pivotal cities of the ancient world. Philippi was anything but heaven; in fact, it was something more of a "hell-hole." Yet, when Paul wrote to the people of Philippi, he called on them not to spite the people around them who were living unworthily, but to love their society by shining the light of the life of the Lord through the quality of the life believers led. Paul's policy—Don't *shoot* at society; *shine* in it. I've learned that some would have us try to save America by spite—by "shooting" at those living beneath our Christian standards. I don't believe that's in the Spirit of Jesus. Let me illustrate.

Last October, I was one of twelve evangelical leaders who accepted an invitation to have breakfast with the President of the United States. The stated agenda of the breakfast meeting was that President Clinton would like to receive "spiritual counsel" from key evangelical leaders. I did not accept this invitation because I was impressed to be asked; neither was I motivated by a quest for political favor. I responded because (1) I'm an American citizen who *could* respond to a President's reasonable request, and because (2) as a leader in the Body of Christ, I was asked for "spiritual counsel."

I'd like to say that in the context of the conversation with the President, that's exactly the way it happened. The meeting was for the purpose we had been led to expect. There was nothing political or manipulative about it—from either side. If there had been, there wasn't a person in the room who wouldn't have seen through it and been repulsed by it.

When I returned, I gave a brief report to my congregation at *The Church On The Way*. I didn't do it because I wanted to call attention to my trip to the White House. I did it because I felt that since the congregation had been praying for the person in the office of President and for the leaders of our land for years, they would care and would want to know what transpired. Though intended only for congregational communication, the tape of my report was spread around and consequently a larger number of people heard about my trip.

As a result of this wide circulation, I was astounded to receive a barrage of angry and critical mail simply because of my willingness to go—to even *consider* breakfast with the President without denouncing him. I'm not complaining about the bludgeoning I received over this meeting. I live in the "kitchen" and I understand the temperature there. However, I want to say that this kind of mail was a sad commentary on how Christian purity is viewed in our country.

Amazingly, many think of "Christian" purity as a separatism that refuses contact or discourse with anyone known to be contrary to one's own biblical lifestyle. (I was also amazed at how many presumed they knew "all" that I'd said, though it was nowhere reported. Some viciously assailed me because I didn't spew a prophecy of judgment in the President's face, even though they still don't know what I *did* say— only having heard what I chose to make public. And I *did* say *more*.)

Nonetheless, the problem appeared in a dramatic way; and to some degree, those who are concerned about Christian purity are right. It's true: we can *never* win the world by lowering ourselves to its standards. Yet, how *do* we disciples of the Lord Jesus live in a sinful world and still reach to it without less than both—love and purity?

Love in purity. How do you do that?

It's clear that some Christians aren't sure how to balance the matters of love and purity. It's *not* easy to walk in Christian purity and still walk openly, reaching a needy world. But we can learn how *not* to compromise standards, while *not* condemning the world around us. Maybe the following will help demonstrate the balance I believe we're to live in.

After my breakfast with the President, I received a letter from a nationally known Christian preacher who had heard that I had been at the White House. He did not say how he felt about it, but it was very clear that he wasn't certain I'd done the right thing.

Here's my response:

"Thank you for your brotherly and biblical approach in inquiring of me concerning the quotation attributed to me by <u>The National Review</u>.

"The sad fact concerning this quotation is not that it misquotes my words (which I'll shortly explain), but that it gives them no context. (Which, as you have sorely discovered, is a common practice of the press!)

"When I was invited to the White House last October, it was in the wake of the President's return from vacation, when he publicly expressed his concern that there was too much "trivialization" of America's people of faith; that it wasn't right that Americans should have to be apologetic about their spiritual convictions.

"The direct agenda of the breakfast meeting was an invitation to 'offer spiritual counsel' in the spirit of the President's new effort at 'hearing' people of evangelical convictions; so I accepted the invitation.

"But hear the qualifiers, please: it was (1) last October, (2) at the time we engaged in conversation, (3) in an environment of genuine openness and seemingly true honesty (which I had no reason to doubt—and I wasn't "swept off my feet" any more than you would have been).

"I cannot account for what he has done since we met. (As to what he had done and said *before*, I had reason to believe his post-vacation words evidenced something was being readied in a man's heart for 'change.' I'm still not sure that's not what he'd like to do, but I'm not close to him and don't know. All I *do* know is that the man I spoke with in October was sincere—not politicizing. I also know that I wasn't duped, nor obligated to be generous for some superficial reason.)"

I further wrote the inquiring televangelist:

"You and I are called to receive people 'taken in adultery' just as Jesus did. When I saw Bill Clinton in October, I wasn't ready to throw any rocks, because I saw a man whom our religious systems had dragged into the arena and were ready (if not already) throwing stones at. I chose to try to hear, and I think I recognized something genuine. If he does or doesn't follow through—if he has or hasn't—isn't something I'm prepared to comment on. The whole Washington, D.C., scene is so shot through with systems that grind people to powder, I'm not going to be too quick to pass a condemning judgment.

"Of course, I *don't* agree with the moral (immoral) positions taken by the President or his advisers or anyone else who violates the standards you and I know are not only righteous in God's eyes, but essential to the survival of nations. But in the middle of all that muddle, I had a moment with a man I treated as an apparently honest man, *seeking*. If I responded in a way that doesn't satisfy those who might criticize my even going when asked, I'm sorry. I've been caught up in trying to follow a Man who is willing to eat with publicans and sinners."

Next, I described to this preacher some of the people who were present at the meeting whose names I won't subject to this public exposure. Their names are already publicly known. The point is that they are people of proven, solid and spiritual good sense. They felt the same things I did; that the President was not "sandbagging," or "schmoozing" us! They felt that he really wanted to know, to hear. That was the context.

That was my answer to an inquiry, questioning whether I may have sacrificed purity in seeking to reach someone—in this case, a president who seems morally ambiguous. But as I said, I've been "caught up" in trying to follow a Man—and that "Man," in case you missed it, is Jesus. Jesus, who was criticized because, though He lived *purely*, He reached *broadly* (see Luke 5:30-32; 7:30-35). And as our text in Philippians instructs, believers are to shine as lights in a dark world. The light can move into *any* darkness, and if fully fueled the light will always win—it's the darkness that has to retreat. So, it is that we're called to be lights today.

And becoming that—in that spirit of holy "reaching" without prudish fear—the people of God will keep pure as they take the steps necessary to "save" America.

STEP 7:

INVADE VIOLENCE

America has become a violent land, inheriting the consequences the Bible prophesies will follow a people who forget God (Ezekiel 8:1-18, note v. 16, 17). It is unnecessary to elaborate the statistics of our bloodshed and domestic brutality, and it is embarrassing to reveal how the nations of our world look with condescent on this feature of our national character. To the whole planet we appear to be a people who conquered their land as "gun-totin' pioneers," only to have our quest for peace violated by drive-by shootings and unnumbered homicides.

From the stormy seas of our cities, which are increasingly tossed by the waves of problem—from gang wars to pollution, from weakened school systems to a deteriorative atmosphere unsupportive of hope for a happy family life—the Church has sought quieter waters. The record of decades is understandable: the emptying of great downtown churches, as parishioners seek the peace and quiet of suburbs, is a pattern of attempted escape. Harried adults seek reprieve, and devoted parents migrate in hopes of preserving a better way of life for their children. Who can blame anyone for the quest for such a haven?

But two facts remain when this effort at escape occurs: (1) the city becomes forsaken by the one entity that can restore her—the living, vital Church; and (2) the relocated Body of Christ tends to lose sight of its mission, and becomes too easily consumed in a Christianity of convenience, rather than becoming a community of redemptive instruments.

However, hope is rising in a number of places today, where *re*-sensitized believers are seeing and accepting the possibility that America can be saved. They know that her cities must be rescued if that prophecy is to become true! As a result, some are envisioning what can happen if a new genre of "city-churches" will rise to reclaim the Church's forsaken mission. Praise God! There *is* being found a cadre of those who, though they live in the suburbs, are still capturing the vision for raising or sustaining a strong congregational voice *within* the city's center. They are committing themselves to serve as members of such vital congregations, for these are people who are convinced of the timeless truth: the Church is constituted of the *redeemed*, called to be *redeemers*, in the Name of *THE Redeemer*. They are the *saved*, committed to *saving* as *THE Savior's servants*.

These are a people through whom America's sorest cities can be healed. They are the people of the Kingdom of God, who know that the *peace* of that Kingdom travels with them, and they have chosen to take it to the center of human strife, rather than run with it to a private haven of comfort. Thank God for these—and all like them who are dedicating themselves to serving the city's need, even in cases where their own homes and family life are removed from the war zone. Thank God that through financial giving, powerful intercession and personal ministry, these have chosen to fight the war of faith to gain "Kingdom" terrain, rather than surrender the city to hell's strategies for human destruction.

Since you care enough to read these words, it's clear that you are one who sees this! I'm thankful for you!! And you and I can partner, from whatever our home base, to see the recovery of America's cities. We are those who have chosen to live in the power and possibilities of this truth: The Church is God's *people*, and His people can win lost cities as well as lost souls.

The living Church is not an institution, but an incarnation of Jesus Christ—His Body, called to enter hell's terrain, not run from its intrusions, to reach with life and love.

> *"And from the days of John the Baptist until now the kingdom of heaven suffers violence, and the violent take it by force."* — *Matthew 11:12*

These words of our Lord Jesus point to the promise of victory amid conflict—of "fighting fire with fire." Jesus is saying that heaven has a countering violence of love that can face and overthrow hellish or human violence which destroys. Let me illustrate:

Every Sunday morning, men from our congregation and another local congregation meet with selected leaders of neighborhood gangs who have asked for help in stopping the killing in the streets of our area. These high-ranking gang leaders represent other gang leaders who control thousands of gang members, children and teenagers in the San Fernando Valley area of Los Angeles.

Their meetings have become effective peace -keeping missions. Gang leaders themselves and their cohorts, tired and weary of the killing, are welcoming godly men who are helping them learn peaceful ways.

Our area newspaper reported that in the last year there's been a twenty-five percent reduction in gang violence in Los Angeles' San Fernando Valley. That didn't just happen because everything turned nice and pretty all of a sudden. It happened because God is doing something. He has done it through people of substance who are invading our city's violence with the love of God. These people have not tried to escape the city, but are partnering together to make a world of difference in the agony-filled center of one of America's largest cities.

This is a dynamic reversal of the history of the American city-church, which has tended to flee the troubled waters of urban turmoil. The pattern of relieving our discomfort by relocating our social setting to a more comfortable clime, is being reshaped. Though the society's commercial and real estate interests have tended to forget the inner-city, an awakened, committed people of faith are re-setting their sights on redemptive possibilities.

Let me add and emphasize the following: I hold no judgment against nor intend any criticism of Christians or churches. I only want to plead with those who *forget*. The fundamental wrong is not in moving to the suburbs or in moving or establishing a church there. What *becomes* crippling to the nation is if those who have relocated either (1) withdraw from serving their city's neediest scenes or (2) remove themselves from action-ministry through churches and agencies who can make a difference in their city.

Personally, I'm privileged as a pastor, serving a "city-church" which is comprised of a host of people committed to serving their city's needs—in every way. Many of our people live in suburbs, while many live within the city's more troubled center. But *all* are committed to a vision for "saving" Los Angeles. As a "Nehemiah Generation," we're targeted on recovering broken people and rebuilding broken communities.

Yes, I am very thankful for a congregation of people who have made a commitment to recognize God has put us where we are—in the center of this part of this city. It's becoming an increasingly tough place to be. But we're not running from it because we believe God has given us a call to work together as a team to invade the need of our city.

I'm also thankful for anybody with that spirit and vision—no matter where they live! It's one of the steps to saving America.

STEP 8:

SERVE THE NEEDY

To "save" America, the living Church needs to capture the moment amid need and crisis in our communities and *serve* the needy.

Serious concern for winning the trust of those you want to reach with the *life* of God recommends you begin by showing them the *love* of God.

The ministry of the Gospel involves compassion for the social need of human-kind, as well as a people's spiritual need. Good works create a platform for gospel truth to be listened to. Jesus said this:

> *"Let your light so shine before men, that they may see your good works and glorify your Father in heaven."* —Matthew 5:16

In these words, our Lord was saying that when you do things to serve a needy world, you gain the right to be heard. People will say of you that you are a person of action who doesn't just "talk the talk," but "walks the walk." There is genuine concern and love evidenced by the way you live and the way you serve others.

In Matthew, Chapter 25, Jesus taught that the day will come when people will stand before Him, and He will have to renounce them. They'll say, "But we did all these wonderful things in Your name, Lord." And He will say that even though they *did* do all those good things, they *still* weren't functioning or serving under His Lordship or in His spirit of love and obedience. He's relating to our taking care of the needy when He says, "When you see the hungry, take them in. When you see the naked, clothe them. When you see those in prison, go and visit them." And as Jesus goes through a lengthy list revealing ways to serve human need, He reinforces the importance of this type of *action*, saying, *"...inasmuch as you did it to one of the least of these My brethren, you did it to Me."*

About four years ago, a team of sixty people in our congregation, who had a deep concern for the enormous spiritual need in an area of our city, set forth a plan. They determined that each week of the month, fifteen of them would take food to a park pavilion in that area and make it available to any individuals or families who would come. The food was provided by surplus groceries received from a local supplier.

When they began, they did or said *nothing* in a direct way that involved the spreading of the Gospel; only saying they were from *The Church On The Way* and wanted to offer these goods as an evidence of our caring.

They did, however, arrive about 30 minutes early each week, in advance of the announced time for food distribution. Upon arrival this group from our church would simply gather in the pavilion and spend 15-20 minutes singing and worshipping the Lord. They didn't ask anyone to join, and they didn't let this hinder their careful preparedness for an on-time distribution of the promised food stuffs.

After about a month, some of the people who were gathering early to stand in line and wait for the distribution asked, "Could we sing and worship with you?—It's so beautiful!" Our people welcomed them doing so...and before long the door was wide open. Without pushing the Gospel in any way, but only presenting the love of God through practical good works, people were asking for more—not only if they could worship, but how they could find peace with God.

Since that time, hundreds have come to Christ through our outreach to that region, and recently a new church was planted in that community. Furthermore, other churches in the area said they have been blessed by our congregation's interest in the people there, and that they are benefiting as well.

Yes! The Gospel *is* the saving "good news," but Jesus said "good works" will open the door to many who need to see to believe. Serving the needy is a very important part of turning a society around. Not only does it answer the immediate need, but it shows that the Church is more than just people who claim to have "the Truth." And serving the needy causes a vastly greater receptivity to the truth we present, giving credence to what we say by the servant spirit that has gained the right to be heard.

STEP 9:
PRESERVE LIBERTY

Earlier in this small book, I lamented the preoccupation many American Christians have with pursuing a political agenda as the focus of their efforts at turning our nation from its pathway of inevitable destruction. Notice, I have not criticized this, only expressed regret for it. I've felt sorry about such preoccupations because of misplaced *priorities*, not because of inappropriate *action*. My regret is that struggling with "flesh" has become substituted for wrestling in prayer against "spirits." Ephesians 6:10-18 draws a clear line of distinctions, which establishes priorities which, if we disregard, will mean inevitable deepening of our frustrations with "flesh" enemies, and an inevitable loss of the battle to *both*—sinful "flesh" and evil "spirits."

Obvious, of course, are instances where some extremist's actions have been so sadly inappropriate, as in the horrifying cases of bombed abortion clinics or assassinated abortionists. Such events, however rare, are a travesty to the cause of whatever righteousness is being sought, and they horribly distort the true mission of people who seek to see God's gracious order kept as a benediction to our land.

However, the preservation of America's true spirit of liberty *does* necessitate taking certain action. The giving, by every Christian, of his or her full attention to their political privileges as a citizen of this free land is *not* less than spiritual. The responsible exercise of our role as Christians, in a nation where (1) freedom of speech, (2) the right to vote, and (3) the privilege of seeking and gaining office are ours to have, needs to be wisely discerned and acted upon. To do these things is not to "wrestle flesh," as long as intercession's priority has been observed.

Let's study this matter by taking time to read these meaty passages of God's Word. They not only describe the *blessings* of good government, but they call for full and faithful *participation* with proper spiritual *priorities*, by those who name the Name of Jesus.

"Let every soul be subject to the governing authorities. For there is no authority except from God, and the authorities that exist are appointed by God.

2 Therefore whoever resists the authority resists the ordinance of God, and those who resist will bring judgment on themselves.

3 For rulers are not a terror to good works, but to evil. Do you want to be unafraid of the authority? Do what is good, and you will have praise from the same.

4 For he is God's minister to you for good. But if you do evil, be afraid; for he does not bear the sword in vain; for he is God's minister, an avenger to execute wrath on him who practices evil.

5 Therefore you must be subject, not only because of wrath but also for conscience' sake.

6 For because of this you also pay taxes, for they are God's ministers attending continually to this very thing.

7 Render therefore to all their due: taxes to whom taxes are due, customs to whom customs, fear to whom fear, honor to whom honor. "

—Romans 13:1-7

"Therefore I exhort first of all that supplications, prayers, intercessions, and giving of thanks be made for all men,

2 for kings and all who are in authority, that we may lead a quiet and peaceable life in all godliness and reverence.

3 For this is good and acceptable in the sight of God our Savior,

4 who desires all men to be saved and to come to the knowledge of the truth." —1 Timothy 2:1-4

These passages are brief, but instructive:

(1) Romans 13 says very clearly that we are to acknowledge the governmental systems under whose authority and governance we live;

(2) First Timothy 2 tells us to pray for all people in authority over us. And, dear friend, remember, these verses were penned during a time when the civilized world was under the carnal and often evil dominion of Rome.

Christians had *no* power of the vote, nor did they have any political right to speak out in that society. Now that we have the privilege, however, we are no less obligated to reveal these attitudes and take these actions—and with proper priority observed.

Intercessory prayer—*with thanksgiving*—is our first and foremost assignment, but *then* the American Christian's privilege of political action *should* be pursued. I see three things we can do to preserve liberty, while still prioritizing intercessory prayer as our first spiritual duty:

1. *Inform ourselves* and *vote*. In our democratic system of government, we are given the *right*—the privilege to vote, but under Christ, I believe, we have also been given the *responsibility* as well. It is my *duty* as a steward of this God-given grace in my free country to make an educated vote. As a disciple of Christ, according to the Scriptures, I am charged to use the gifts Divine providence gives me. The right to vote certainly is in that category! *No*, God's kingdom *isn't* of this world, *but He has put you and me in it!* And He's called us to be instruments who make a difference in this world. Voting can do that!

    It is each Christian citizen's prerogative to decide how he or she votes. I never tell people how to vote. However, I do explain local or state propositions that have to do with moral issues or things that can become destructive to our culture. I refuse to declare anything of political partisanship, and I will *not* publicly *attack* a political leader or his policies. I *will* lead in prayer when known issues are at stake or when certain leaders dismay or fail us. But I don't believe it's my calling to tell people how to vote. However, given this right, we should vote—with understanding and discernment.

2. Secondly, you have the right to *lift your voice* and state your opinion: "Ours is a free society. While simply raising a protest for protest's sake has no value, a sensible, clear-eyed communication with a Congressman, legislator, city councilman, or a member of your county board of supervisors, *does* have its value. It's something that is our privilege and call to do.

I will also often encourage people to write their governmental representatives. And though I refuse to attack people or their policies in public, I will express my concerns in pointed and forthright correspondence. Further, I forthrightly proclaim the truth of God over the airwaves—and that truth will at times address issues that call *everyone*— including those who govern—to hear God's Word as He reveals how we are to live and love in this world. Let me urge you, too.

"Lift your voice" through writing timely letters! By this, I mean, write a letter that sounds like it is coming from an intelligent, informed, caring, and loving person who is interested in the welfare of a nation, not just in spewing bigoted ideas with rancor. To write an angry letter in a defiant spirit wins nothing. But to communicate with the wisdom of God and in the spirit of Jesus is a privilege we have, when exercised biblically, and it is not to be taken lightly.

3. Thirdly, our political freedom affords the privilege of *seeking the responsibility of governmental office*. If this is within your gifting and your sense of mission, to involve yourself in government, I encourage you to go for it! However, do it because you're a capable person who sensible people can trust and a judicious person with well-informed convictions. Don't run for office just because you're a Christian and hope to appeal to people to support you "because I'm a Christian."

Because a person is a Christian does not necessarily make him or her a better public servant than anyone else. Sure, any Christians are better than any non-Christians in the respect that they can have a lot happier life right now, and certainly have a lot more joyous eternity! But being a Christian doesn't mean a person is necessarily ready or better equipped for the task of governing. However, if you have God's gifting and Christ's calling and a Holy Spirit vision for serving your society, God will make you able for the task!

I believe God is looking for people who want to be instruments of His in the political arena. And the preservation of America's liberties will be assured—America *saved* from political bondage—when righteous people *serve* their land as faithful citizens and honest taxpayers. It's still true today:

"Righteousness exalts a nation, but sin is a reproach to any people" (Proverbs 14:34), and,

"When the righteous are in authority, the people rejoice; But when a wicked man rules, the people groan" (Proverbs 29:2).

STEP 10:

DEMONSTRATE, DECLARE, AND DISPENSE THE GOSPEL

"But where sin abounded, grace abounded much more." —Romans 5:20

Finally, to move forward toward saving America, we need to spread the Gospel. To leave this to last is not to diminish its importance, but to accentuate it. And it's also to make clear that our gospel will be more readily received and believed if we've done the other nine things *first!* So, as living evidences of the Resurrected Savior, who *demonstrate* Him, let us be *evangelizing* people—who *declare* His truth with winsomeness and *dispense* His power in His Name as the Holy Spirit fills us for the task.

This tenth step is the most obvious, of course. And I don't need to belabor this point because every believer knows this needs to be done. Our perspective is clear: Our primary mission is to evangelize lost souls. Ultimately, THAT is how America will be *saved.*

Yes, we help the needy at our church. Every

week *thousands* of dollars flow out from the congregation to help people in our city who are in social need. *But,* above and beyond that, we also *spread the Gospel,* for we spend *tens of thousands* of dollars every week to minister God's Word everywhere. We "give away" nearly two million dollars annually for home and foreign missions and other gospel outreaches. Our foremost task is to spread the Word, and we do it!

I'm sure you are aware that there's more to this point than our giving the funds needed to reach souls for Christ. As important as that is, it is my deepest desire to see people mobilized—through a Christlike, discipled character, joined to a warmhearted motivation—to demonstrate the Gospel with grace and good sense. Spreading the Gospel has to do with the power of the Spirit of God being manifest in your life. It doesn't have to do with posturing yourself by making pompous declarations or spouting religious noises. Rather, it has to do with something of substance going on *in* you, so that wherever you walk, Jesus' footprints are left behind as the marks you've made in your circle of influence. Let me describe what I mean by "people of substance."

OUR CALL

Several years ago, Anna and I had a free day in Jerusalem—that incredible city of such wondrous historic and prophetic significance to us all. As we were planning our day, we decided to pursue the path of "the ascent of Olives;" a roadway which moves from the Eastern Gate of the Old City, up the slopes of the

Mount of Olives, and eastward toward Bethany, about four miles away.

It was a hot, dusty day, and once we had crested the hill we were both perspiring and feeling tempted to return to our hotel because we still had miles to go to our goal in Bethany. But with dogged determination, we proceeded. We've always been glad we did.

A single stone pillar may not seem much of a reward to some people, especially after having pressed on through with such a hike. But we were delighted to make a "find," just a short distance from the traditional ancient site of Lazarus' tomb. It was a Roman *milestone.*

In Roman times, a network of highways was constructed throughout the Empire, facilitating travel and linking the vast realm of Rome's rule in a way that expedited commerce as well as assured quick movement of the emperor's troops if needed anywhere to quell civil disturbances. Such pillars as the one we found that day, beyond the top of Mt. Olivet, were common in those days—and here was one, right before our eyes.

It was fascinating for historical and archaeological reasons—about six feet tall and about three feet in circumference. And while all it was used for was to mark the *way* and to indicate *distance* traveled, my imagination was completely captivated. I saw a dramatic parallel.

That parallel comes to mind right now, as I draw toward the conclusion of this book with you. I saw how a *single pillar* could be *so significant*, and for *so long a time*, simply by standing tall and strong. It occurred to me: "Here is a picture of what God wants each of His people to be." See the picture:

1. Let the Lord make you a *pillar*, as you "overcome" by faith and *stand tall* and *strong* for Christ (Revelation 3:12).

2. Let your presence *point the way* for others to find THE WAY (John 14:6), and remain constant "without falling" so your witness abides with the passing of time (Jude 14, 25).

As you and I do this, we don't need to launch crusades or wave flags—we simply need to *be there*. There are multitudes passing by, and a faithful *pillar person* will become a trusted point of reference, and people will be pointed to Christ.

As we learn to live this way and pray God's way; with the force of His love animating us, we cannot only change our land, but we can create a climate that the Bible says will magnificently provide for an atmosphere in which people will be saved. Remember, 1 Timothy 2:1-4, which exhorts that our first priority is to pray, says such prayer by faith-filled people will bring "a quiet and peaceable life," and in that atmosphere, people will "be saved and come to the knowledge of the truth."

Dear ones, stand strong and tall. Pray for those who are in government. Pray for those who are in ruling positions; that is, not only people in political office, but those in many different arenas: finance, entertainment, business, education, industry, church life, etc. And remember, we pray for these people *not* because they're important, but because they are *needy*.

And according to God's Word, pray with *thankfulness* (1 Timothy 4:1; Philippians 4:6). Let *that* spirit of gratitude fill your heart—even when leaders frustrate you by their words and actions. For example, when was the last time you *thanked* God for our President and his Cabinet? When was the last time you *thanked* God for the Surgeon General? When was the last time you *thanked* God for military leadership?

We may not have reason to be thankful for all that is represented by some of these people, or said by them, but we *can* thank the Lord that we live in a land where there is freedom, and where we can publicly worship, even as we pray for our leaders. We *can* thank Him that His Word says "the heart of the king is in the hand of the Lord" (Proverbs 21:1).

And above all, thank God that His hand is moved by the prayers of His people! God doesn't need the anger of an enraged group of saints who feel their standards have been violated, but the compassion and fiery intercession of those who see how *hell* has intruded upon our land. Focus the right enemy, and come before your Friend in heaven with faith!

Let's rise with a new belief that He will hear us when we sing, "God bless America, land that I love...Stand beside her and guide her, through the night with a light from above…God bless America, my home, sweet home."

America can be saved! And what it takes to make that change is for people, with hearts that hurt for a torn-up world, to pray with a passion. Let's move together as people who pray:

"Lord, I welcome You to come upon me, to fill me, and to move in and through me so that I will be a person who moves with wisdom, in the glory of God. Fill me with 'the right stuff'—with what it takes to live and apply these ten steps to save America. And, Lord, as You live Your life in and through me, may I be a pillar person pointing the Way, and may Your footsteps be seen where I have walked and served in my needy nation."

Amen.

Notes

Notes

_____
_____
_____
_____
_____
_____
_____
_____
_____
_____
_____
_____
_____
_____
_____
_____
_____
_____
_____
_____
_____
_____
_____

Notes

Notes

Notes

Notes

Notes

Notes

Additional Ministry Resources:

PRAYER IS INVADING THE IMPOSSIBLE

To Jack Hayford, prayer is not the mystical experience of a few special people, but an aggressive act in the face of impossibility—an act that may be performed by anyone who will accept the challenge to learn to pray.

Hardcover **PIIHC** '12.95
Paperback **PII02** '7.95
Spanish Paperback Edition **SPPI** '4.95

INVADING THE IMPOSSIBLE THROUGH PRAYER AND FASTING

These three audio teachings will reveal fasting as an instrument of spiritual power, a key by which bonds of evil are broken, and a means by which God's counsel is received and established in the affairs of men. This dynamic trio of teachings will release you to experience spiritual triumph and practical service for Christ's Kingdom. **Audio Album SC450** '13.00

I'LL HOLD YOU IN HEAVEN

This best-selling book answers the heart-cry of many faced with the ordeal of walking through the questions, the fears, the doubts, and the uncertainties of parents of the stillborn, miscarried, or aborted. The freeing truth of the Word of God takes the reader beyond the hurts and into the hope of eternity. *Regularly* '4.95 **HYH** '3.95

TEN STEPS TOWARD SAVING AMERICA

The teaching series by Pastor Jack Hayford—from which this book has been adapted—is available on audio or video tape, and it comes packaged with a copy of this helpful handbook of the teaching. Additional copies of this book may be purchased separately. Ten Steps Toward Saving America stresses that people whose faith and action are rooted in God's call and promises can determine the destiny of nations. *2-Tape Audio Album & book/* SC510 $10
VHS Video & book/ V3897 $20 • *Book /*TSTSA $3.95

PRAYERS THAT PREVAIL...for America
(Changing a Nation Through Prayer)

Prayers That Prevail...for America is a user-friendly tool for every believer who is concerned about our nation. It shows how prevailing prayer will bring lasting change to our land. The focus of this practical handbook is on God's promises rather than America's problems. The reader is thereby fortified for victorious intercession, by learning how to pray God's Word for our country, our leaders, and our people. God will bless America as His people learn to put the prayer principles of His Word into action through dynamic intercession!

PPA $9

TOUCHING YOUR TOWN THRU' PRAYER

The two tapes in this small album will teach you how to touch and transform your town for God.   SC393 $8

THE WAR IN YOUR LIFE AND WORLD

This 2-tape album presents a biblical challenge to be people of prayer and endurance. **SC367 $8**

OUTRACING THE WORLD:
"An Appeal to Transethnicity"

In this candid and forthright series, Pastor Hayford shares his own testimony of God's changing his heart about unperceived prejudice in the light of God's Word and the love of God's Spirit. You will want to have the full, extended presentations of these landmark messages. The audio album contains three tapes, and the special VHS video features nearly three hours of teaching. Each comes with a complimentary copy of helpful outlines and added study notes.

Audio Album SC488 '13
VHS/V3803 '25

HEALING AMERICA'S WOUNDS

In this powerful book, John Dawson shows how the open wounds of our past and present are bleeding the life from America. Discover how you can play a part in breaking the chain of sin that has been handed down from generation to generation. Healing America's Wounds will stir you to action and help you find the faith to seek God's plan for you in the reconciliation of a divided America. **HAW '10.99**

CHURCHES THAT PRAY

Peter Wagner reveals how prayer can help revitalize your congregation and break down the walls between your church and your community. You'll learn why God often waits for our prayers before He acts, and you'll discover how you and others can pray with more power.

CTP '15.99

PRAYERS THAT PREVAIL FOR YOUR CHILDREN

This exciting new release is a practical manual of prayers for parents and grandparents to use as they pray for the precious children in their families. More than 80 topical prayers of intercession are included to serve as models for Bible based, effective praying for our children. Each of the Scriptural prayers focuses on the promises of God rather than the problems of life. In addition to the prayers, the book contains teaching that will help parents fulfill their calling, and a prayer journal that enables the reader to keep a record of God's faithful answers to our prayers for our children. **PTCP '8.99**

POSSESSING THE GATES OF THE ENEMY

Cindy Jacobs provides a unique training manual for militant intercession: "invading" countries, covering them with prayer, and engaging in spiritual warfare. Whether you are a beginning "pray-er" or an experienced intercessor, you can learn to pray about the concerns and matters that are on the heart of God—and possess the gates of the enemy. **PGE '9.95**

Please add 15% to all orders for shipping/handling.
California residents, add 8.25% tax.

ORDER FORM

Qty.	Item	Code	Price	Total
____	_____	___	___	___
____	_____	___	___	___
____	_____	___	___	___
____	_____	___	___	___
____	_____	___	___	___
____	_____	___	___	___
____	_____	___	___	___
____	_____	___	___	___
____	_____	___	___	___
____	_____	___	___	___
____	_____	___	___	___
____	_____	___	___	___
____	_____	___	___	___

Postage and Handling
$0.00 - $9.99 . . . . $2.00
$10.00 - $29.99 . . . . $4.00
$30.00 - $49.99 . . . . $6.00
$50.00 and up . . . . 15% of subtotal
All orders outside the USA. . $3. min,
or 20% of Subtotal

Subtotal _____

Add 8.25% sales tax to CA orders _____

Shipping and Handling _____

Donation (Optional) _____

Total _____

Name _____

Street Address _____

City _____ State _____ Zip_____

Phone Number (_____) _____

Method of Payment: ❏ Check or Money Order ❏ Visa ❏ MC

_____/ _____-_____-_____-_____/ _____
Signature   Card Number   Exp. Date

RESOURCES   14820 Sherman Way, Van Nuys, CA 91405-2233
1-800-776-8180 • 1-818-779-8480

Please include your remittance (U.S. currency only) with order.
Make check or money order payable to Living Way Ministries.